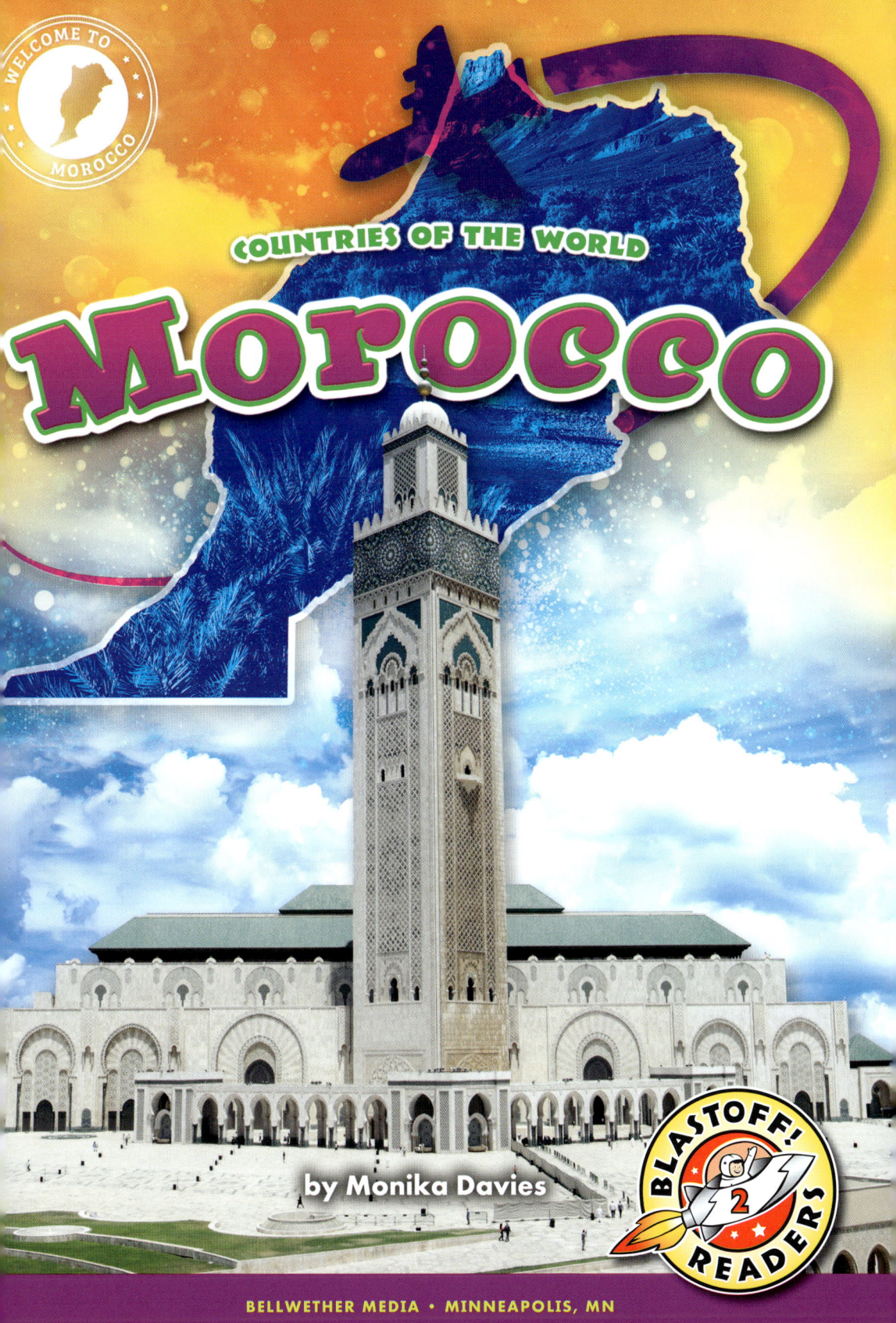

Blastoff! Readers are carefully developed by literacy experts to build reading stamina and move students toward fluency by combining standards-based content with developmentally appropriate text.

Level 1 provides the most support through repetition of high-frequency words, light text, predictable sentence patterns, and strong visual support.

Level 2 offers early readers a bit more challenge through varied sentences, increased text load, and text-supportive special features.

Level 3 advances early-fluent readers toward fluency through increased text load, less reliance on photos, advancing concepts, longer sentences, and more complex special features.

★ **Blastoff! Universe**

Reading Level

Grade K

Grades 1–3

Grade 4

This edition first published in 2024 by Bellwether Media, Inc.

No part of this publication may be reproduced in whole or in part without written permission of the publisher. For information regarding permission, write to Bellwether Media, Inc., Attention: Permissions Department, 6012 Blue Circle Drive, Minnetonka, MN 55343.

Library of Congress Cataloging-in-Publication Data

Names: Davies, Monika, author.
Title: Morocco / by Monika Davies.
Other titles: Blastoff! readers. 2, Countries of the world.
Description: Minneapolis, MN : Bellwether Media, Inc., 2024. | Series: Blastoff! Readers: countries of the world | Includes bibliographical references and index. | Audience: Ages 5-8 | Audience: Grades 2-3 | Summary: "Relevant images match informative text in this introduction to Morocco. Intended for students in kindergarten through third grade"–Provided by publisher.
Identifiers: LCCN 2023046582 (print) | LCCN 2023046583 (ebook) | ISBN 9798886877960 (library binding) | ISBN 9798886878905 (ebook)
Subjects: LCSH: Morocco–Juvenile literature.
Classification: LCC DT305 .D38 2024 (print) | LCC DT305 (ebook) | DDC 964–dc23/eng/20231005
LC record available at https://lccn.loc.gov/2023046582
LC ebook record available at https://lccn.loc.gov/2023046583

Text copyright © 2024 by Bellwether Media, Inc. BLASTOFF! READERS and associated logos are trademarks and/or registered trademarks of Bellwether Media, Inc.

Editor: Rachael Barnes   Designer: Gabriel Hilger

Printed in the United States of America, North Mankato, MN.

Table of Contents

All About Morocco	4
Land and Animals	6
Life in Morocco	12
Morocco Facts	20
Glossary	22
To Learn More	23
Index	24

All About Morocco

Rabat

Morocco is in the northwest corner of Africa. Its capital is Rabat.

Outdoor markets are in most cities. They are called *souks*. People sell everything from food to shoes!

Land and Animals

The Atlas Mountains cut across central Morocco. **Plains** line the west coast.

The Sahara **Desert** covers the south and east.

Atlas Mountains

Sahara Desert

Size: around 3,320,000 square miles (8,598,761 square kilometers)

Famous For: the world's largest desert

winter

Winters are warm and rainy. Summers are hot and dry.

Hot, dusty winds blow in the desert. Ocean breezes cool the **coastal** plains.

desert wind

Many animals call Morocco home. Geckos rest on warm mountain rocks. Sand cats hunt in the desert.

sand cat

Animals of Morocco

Atlas day gecko

sand cat

white stork

greater flamingo

Storks build nests on city rooftops. Flamingos fly near water.

Life in Morocco

Moroccans are often **Arabs** or **Berbers**. Nearly all Moroccans are **Muslims**. Arabic is widely spoken. Many people are **bilingual**.

Most people live in cities. Casablanca is the biggest.

Casablanca

soccer

Moroccans love to watch and play soccer. Tennis and golf are also popular.

Many people go to **festivals**. Families visit the beach on weekends. They swim and have picnics!

festival

B'stilla is a Moroccan meat pastry. Couscous is a small pasta. It is paired with stew.

Moroccan Foods

b'stilla

couscous

b'ssara

mint tea

B'ssara is a bean soup.
Mint tea is a favorite drink!

Throne Day

Throne Day is in July. Moroccans honor their king. Many wear white. They watch parades.

Muslims **fast** for Ramadan.
It ends with *Eid al-Fitr*.
Families gather to eat and pray.

Morocco Facts

Size:
276,662 square miles
(716,551 square kilometers)

Population:
37,067,420 (2023)

National Holiday:
Throne Day (July 30)

Main Languages:
Arabic and Tamazight

Capital City:
Rabat

Famous Face

Name: Nadir Khayat

Famous For: musician, producer, and songwriter known as RedOne

Religions

other: 1%   Muslim 99%

Top Landmarks

Hassan II Mosque

Jemaa el-Fna Square

Sahara Desert

Glossary

Arabs—people who live mostly in the Middle East and northern Africa

Berbers—people who are originally from northwestern Africa

bilingual—can speak and understand two languages

coastal—near the shore

desert—dry land with few plants and little rainfall

fast—to stop eating all or some foods for a certain period of time

festivals—events of celebration

Muslims—people of the Islamic faith; Muslims follow the teachings of Muhammad as told to him from Allah.

plains—large areas of flat land

To Learn More

AT THE LIBRARY

Ferguson, Melissa. *Ramadan and Eid al-Fitr*. North Mankato, Minn.: Pebble, 2021.

Gish, Melissa. *Storks*. Mankato, Minn.: Creative Education, 2024.

Spanier, Kristine. *Morocco*. Minneapolis, Minn.: Jump!, 2021.

ON THE WEB

Factsurfer.com gives you a safe, fun way to find more information.

1. Go to www.factsurfer.com.

2. Enter "Morocco" into the search box and click 🔍.

3. Select your book cover to see a list of related content.

Index

Africa, 4
animals, 10, 11
Arabic, 12, 13
Arabs, 12
Atlas Mountains, 6, 10
beach, 15
Berbers, 12
bilingual, 12
capital (see Rabat)
Casablanca, 12
cities, 5, 11, 12
coast, 6, 9
Eid al-Fitr, 19
fast, 19
festivals, 15
food, 5, 16, 17
golf, 14
map, 5
markets, 5
Morocco facts, 20–21

Muslims, 12, 19
people, 5, 12, 14, 15, 18, 19
plains, 6, 9
Rabat, 4, 5
Ramadan, 19
Sahara Desert, 6, 7, 9, 10
say hello, 13
soccer, 14
summers, 8
tennis, 14
Throne Day, 18
winds, 9
winters, 8

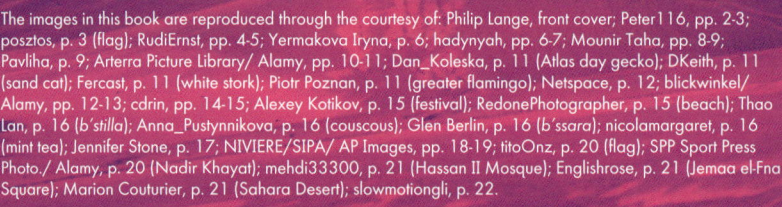

The images in this book are reproduced through the courtesy of: Philip Lange, front cover; Peter116, pp. 2-3; posztos, p. 3 (flag); RudiErnst, pp. 4-5; Yermakova Iryna, p. 6; hadynyah, pp. 6-7; Mounir Taha, pp. 8-9; Pavliha, p. 9; Arterra Picture Library/ Alamy, pp. 10-11; Dan_Koleska, p. 11 (Atlas day gecko); DKeith, p. 11 (sand cat); Fercast, p. 11 (white stork); Piotr Poznan, p. 11 (greater flamingo); Netspace, p. 12; blickwinkel/ Alamy, pp. 12-13; cdrin, pp. 14-15; Alexey Kotikov, p. 15 (festival); RedonePhotographer, p. 15 (beach); Thao Lan, p. 16 (*b'stilla*); Anna_Pustynnikova, p. 16 (couscous); Glen Berlin, p. 16 (*b'ssara*); nicolamargaret, p. 16 (mint tea); Jennifer Stone, p. 17; NIVIERE/SIPA/ AP Images, pp. 18-19; titoOnz, p. 20 (flag); SPP Sport Press Photo./ Alamy, p. 20 (Nadir Khayat); mehdi33300, p. 21 (Hassan II Mosque); Englishrose, p. 21 (Jemaa el-Fna Square); Marion Couturier, p. 21 (Sahara Desert); slowmotiongli, p. 22.